365

REASONS

Why I'm Still

SINGLE

Printed in China

9 8 7 6 5 4 3 2 1
Digit on the right indicates the number of this printing

Library of Congress Control Number:2009943400

ISBN 978-0-7624-3788-7

Running Press Book Publishers
2300 Chestnut Street
Philadelphia, PA 19103-4371

Visit us on the web!
www.runningpress.com

365

REASONS
Why I'm Still
SINGLE

Michele Alexander
and Jeannie Long

Running Press
PHILADELPHIA • LONDON

1.

I like variety:
it's the spice of life.

2.

My psychic told me I
haven't met "the one" yet.

3.

I've never been
a planner.

4.
People bug me.

5.
My calendar is already jam-packed.

6.
My fear of commitment outweighs my willingness to settle.

7.

I'm fine with the richer, but not the poorer.

Perfect excuse:
for your online dating profile

8.
I like my freedom.

9.
I lost a bet.

10.
Forty is the new twenty.

11.

Guys are intimidated
by my beauty.

12.

I'm a germ-a-phobe.

13.

I'm a lifezilla; being a
bridezilla would be
a downgrade.

14

Forever is a lot
longer than it used
to be.

Perfect excuse:
for your grandma

15.

I'm bringing spinster back.

16.

I'm a one-upper.

17.

I've complained so much
about other people's
weddings, I can't live up to
my own expectations.

18.

I've followed *The Rules*, but
it only works on **assholes**
(and guys I don't like).

19.

Hollywood endings
have ruined real-life love
for me.

20.

I give up too **soon**.

21.

I'm tall; I can reach everything I need.

Perfect excuse:
for the dude with the
Napoleon complex

22.

I'm a lone ranger.

23.

Marriage is overrated.

24.

I haven't climbed
Mt. Kilimanjaro yet.

25.

I still live at home.

26.

I ride a unicycle.

27.

I need the closet space.

28.

My life isn't a
democracy, there's
only one vote
that counts.

Perfect excuse: on Election Day

29.
I can make a short story long.

30.
I've never caught the bouquet.

31.
I'm a stalker.
One date and I can't resist a drive-by.

32.

I'm just not ready yet.

33.

I'm not at liberty
to say.

34.

I give away the milk
for free.

35.

I'm always in the
"friend zone."

Perfect excuse: for the guy
you are trying to
"form a relationship with"

36.

I'm waiting
for a sign.

37.

I'm not any good
at dirty talk.

38.

I'm married to my job.

39.

I'm not even looking.

40.

I'm always invited because I don't have "the old ball-and-chain" tagging along.

41.

I don't want to have or to hold.

42.

There aren't enough self-help books in the world to help me with my issues.

Perfect excuse: for people that say, "You're so cute—why are you still single?"

43.
It's so cliché.

44.
I don't want to give up hot vacation romances.

45.
Anything more than a one-night stand is overkill.

46.
I wear
granny panties.

47.
I _am_ the sharpest tool
in the shed.

48.
I'm way too honest
on my online profile.

49.

Single is the new married.

Perfect excuse:
in a marketing meeting

50.
"Marriage" is code for "slavery."

51.
I'm a hoarder; I don't have the room.

52.
I have my own personality.

53.

So many men,
so little time.

54.

The guys I meet
are stupid.

55.

There's only room for
one numero uno.

56.

I'm on strike.

Perfect excuse: when your mom
tries to set you up with her friend's
lonely son for the umpteenth time

57.
I'm in love with myself.

58.
Nobody
understands me.

59.
"Domestic bliss"
is a myth.

60.
I have more important
things to do.

61.
I have no patience.

62.
I peaked
in high school.

63.

Being single
is the new "green."

Perfect excuse:
for do-gooders

64.

There's no "I" in "we."

65.

I'm allergic to
testosterone.

66.

I'm a non-conformist.

67.

I have an ego problem.

68.

It's a self-fulfilling
prophecy.

69.

I've been trying to manifest
a husband using my vision
board, but it just hasn't
worked yet.

70.

I don't talk to strangers.

Perfect excuse:
for your diary

71.
The longer I wait, the more special it will be.

72.
My "deal breaker" list is extremely long.

73.
I still answer booty calls.

74.

I still have my own opinion.

75.

I pave my own way.

76.

I don't need a man.

77.

It really IS you
and not me.

Perfect excuse for:
you know who you are!

78.

I couldn't stand to
spend that much time
with one person.

79.

The only "we" I'm
interested in is
a game console.

80.

I have body dysmorphia.

81.

I still haven't found
what I'm looking for.

82.

Too much risk,
too little reward.

83.

Turns out, I am the
biggest loser.

84.

One-night stands
are still on the table.

Perfect excuse: backstage

85.

I'm at my sexual peak,
why waste it on one guy?

86.

I can manage my own
finances.

87.

I'm holding out
for a hero.

88.

I'm way too talented.

89.

I'm just not that
into you.

90.

I'm waiting for
Clooney.

01.

I still like random
sex with strangers.

Perfect excuse:
at an engagement party

92.

I got rejected by
e-Harmony.

93.

My therapist says
I'm too co-dependent.

94.

I've had a couple close
calls, but nothing's
"stuck" yet.

95.
I'm afraid of making a mistake.

96.
Who wants to be tied down on Presidents' Day?

97.
I peaked in middle school.

98.

I have a hard enough
time locking into a
cell phone plan
for 2 years.

**Perfect excuse:
for your therapist**

99.
My softball teammates never approve of any guys I meet...for some reason.

100.
I don't want to lose my personality.

101.
It's not on my to-do list.

102.
It's too complicated.

103.
I'm a flake.

104.
I have restless leg
syndrome.

105.

I'd rather get
a pony.

Perfect excuse:
for your dad

116.

I relate to the
Golden Girls.

117.

I'm too funny.

118.

I haven't figured out
how to trick a guy
into it.

119.

I just need to lose
10 more pounds.

Perfect excuse:
at your weigh-in

120.
I'm too lazy.

121.
I'm too pretty.

122.
I'm too important.

123.

I'm too opinionated.

124.

I'm too perfect.

125.

I'm too picky.

126.

I like me.

Perfect excuse: it makes little sense to married folk but continues to have credence for you

127.

I have a checkered past
. . . and present.

128.

I look terrible in white.

129.

I have unrealistic
expectations.

130.

I wouldn't want to raise
the divorce rate.

131.

No one gets my humor.

132.

Nobody returns
my phone calls.

133.

I like assholes.

Perfect excuse:
for a run-in with your ex

134.

Unless he shows up at my door, I'm never going to meet him.

135.

I don't like to share food.

136.

I'm always right.

137.

I'd lose my Nielsen
standing.

138.

I promised myself
I wouldn't.

139.

I just moved here.

140.

I'm in the witness protection program.

Perfect excuse:
on a solo vacation

141.
I'm kind of a big deal.

142.
I would do a lot
for a Klondike bar . . .
but I won't do that.

143.
My pictures on my
online profile don't look
anything like me.

144.

I fear halitosis.

145.

I don't need anyone else
telling me what to do.

146.

I don't want a
"dirty" diamond.

147.

I spent the last year at a silent retreat; it's been tough getting back into regular life.

Perfect excuse:
for your life coach

148.
P.M.S.

149.
I actually prefer
being single.

150.
Sex with the same
person is boring.

151.
Sharing isn't my forte.

152.
I wouldn't **have** time
to **tweet**.

153.
I shotgun beer.

154.

I still got it!

Perfect excuse:
on the dance floor

155.
At this point, why bother?

156.
The last thing I need is another mouth to feed.

157.
There are no single guys worthy of me.

158.

You can always go to the
front of the line as
a "single rider."

159.

I'm lovin' it . . .
all by myself.

160.

I peaked in
kindergarten.

161.

I was actually
thinking of moving
back home.

Perfect excuse:
for your parents

162.

I'm more like Mars
than Venus.

163.

I guess they just don't
make "shining armor"
like they used to.

164.

I hate labels.

165.
I'm a late bloomer.

166.
I wear the pants.

167.
For me,
commitment = death.

168.

I would gain too
much weight.

Perfect excuse: for your newly
overweight married friends

169.

I'm tan-o-rexic.

170.

I don't want to flake on
my other single friends.

171.

I'm holding out
for a sugar daddy.

172.

I won't make anyone
feel superior.

173.

I hate weddings.

174.

I listen to my friends'
bad relationship advice.

175.

I'm all drama.

Perfect excuse:
at a job interview

176.

Give me five minutes and I can find something wrong with anyone.

177.

I'm kind of a downer.

178.

Nobody likes me for that long.

179.
I don't like being the center of attention.

180.
Living in sin sounds more exciting.

181.
You don't have to get married anymore.

182.

I'm super-busy.

183.

It's none of your business.

184.

I don't need any more drama in my life.

185.

I don't need anyone else bragging about me.

186.

I fart in my sleep.

187.

I fear the unknown.

188.

I guess it just wasn't
"meant to be."

189.

I'm addicted to me.

190.

I've noticed that
I'm only really happy
when I'm alone.

191.

I sometimes say
things like,
"What's crack-a-lackin?"

192.

I have
an annoying laugh.

193.
I live with a gay man.

194.
I love 'em and leave 'em.

195.
I'm selfish in bed.

196.
I can't follow directions.

197.

I don't need someone all up in my grill.

Perfect excuse: for a close talker at Home Depot

198.

I have no follow-
through.

199.

I'm not gonna lie:
I have a lot of junk
in my trunk.

200.

I just wanna have fun.

201.
I know too much
about football.

202.
I refuse to do someone
else's laundry.

203.
I have B.O.

2024.

Social networking
has ruined what
little game I had.

Perfect excuse: on Facebook

205.
I'm caught in
a time warp.

206.
I do the Time Warp.

207.
I'm not finished with
my lesbian phase yet.

208.
I'd rather be single
than be with (insert your
husband's name here).

209.
I haven't had a religious
experience yet.

210.
I haven't met my
Prince Charming.

211.

I'm waiting until the gays have the right to marry.

Perfect excuse: at Gay Pride

212.
I just don't want to.

213.
I refuse to move.

214.
I don't need
the added
responsibility.

215.

I spoon my dog.

216.

I'm still in my
"bad boy" phase.

217.

I sweat
the small stuff.

218.

I can't decide
between the
chicken and fish.

Perfect Excuse: at a wedding

219.
I don't want
to change.

220.
I don't want
to grow up.

221.
I've been preoccupied.

222.
I don't believe in
soulmates.

223.
I like to remain
a mystery.

224.
I can never get past
the 3-month hump.

225.

I'm still relevant.

Perfect excuse: for all the
popular girls from high school

226.

I watch too much
reality TV.

227.

I hog the bed.

228.

I just broke up
with someone.

229.
I don't believe in
"the one."

230.
I can't find anyone
smart enough.

231.
I can't stand snoring.

232.

Have you seen what's out there?

Perfect excuse:
at a cougar convention

233.
Monogamy is boring.

234.
I've been to paradise, but
I've never been to me.

235.
I don't want to miss out
on a whole new generation
of guys just graduating
college.

236.

I've never thought
about it.

237.

My friends are so clue-
less; they won't set me
up with anyone.

238.

My standards are
way too high.

239.

I'm too smart.

Perfect excuse: for every guy
who's married

240.

I prefer the road less traveled.

241.

I'm too cool.

242.

The guys I meet online have way too much baggage.

243.

There is less stuff to fill out on applications.

244.

I'm gassy.

245.

I'm having WAY too much fun.

246.

I'm waiting on my intellectual equal.

Perfect excuse:
at the DMV

247.

I like to come and go
as I please.

248.

I'm a neat freak.
I couldn't live with
someone else.

249.

I'm geographically
undesirable.

250

The timing is off.

251

It's more fun to check "single" on applications.

252

I wear my sunglasses at night.

253.

The grass really <u>is</u> greener.

Perfect excuse:
at a baby shower

254.

I'm not a good flirt.

255.

I'm on a mission
from God.

256.

I only like
missionary.

257.

I'm being patient. I have a 50/50 chance that one of the good ones won't be taken for too much longer.

258.

I read Harlequin romance novels.

259.

I want to travel.

260.

My parents' marriage scarred me for life.

Perfect excuse:
at a family reunion

261.

I have no game.

262.

I'm a
"glass half empty"
type of person.

263.

I'm a ball-buster.

264.
I'm a sexist.

265.
I'm a rebel.

266.
I have
really bad taste
in men.

267.

I'm afraid of love.

Perfect excuse:
on Valentine's Day

268.
My single friends sabotage all my relationships.

269.
My feet smell.

270.
My friends are more fun.

271.
I come first.

272.
My hammock
is made for one.

273.
My maid already
takes out the trash.

2724.

I'm already in a
dysfunctional relationship
with my boss.

Perfect excuse:
for human resources

275.
I just don't have
the time.

276.
I'm a crazy cat lady.

277.
It would stifle my
creativity.

278.

I'm still not over my
Lance Bass obsession.

279.

What was the question
again?

280.

I'm a free spirit.

281.

I'm too self-absorbed.

Perfect excuse: for your friends that tell you that you are "too self-absorbed"

282.

One is my favorite
number.

283.

One is NOT
the loneliest number.

284.

It's not in my
10-year plan.

285.

You can't always get
what you want.

286.

You can't ever count
on me.

287.

I'm not a closer.

88.

I don't like change.

Perfect excuse:
for Republicans

289.

I answer to no one.

290.

I talk openly about
bowel movements.

291.

I think I can always
do better.

292.

I can out-drink
most guys.

293.

I think for myself.

294.

I can't cook.

295.

It's not on my
bucket list.

**Perfect excuse:
at a funeral**

296.
I'm afraid
I'd miss out on
something better.

297.
I'm fickle.

298.
**Everyone I know
is gay.**

299.

Everyone else is boring.

300.

"Going to the Chapel" is quite possibly the most annoying song ever.

301.

It's my prerogative!

302.

Jesus is
my soulmate.

Perfect excuse:
in church

303.
The tax break isn't
a big enough incentive.

304.
I don't need anyone
else judging me.

305.
My promise ring
is stuck.

306.
I never compromise.

307.
I'm celibate.

308.
I judge guys
based on their
status updates.

309.

My credit score is too good.

Perfect excuse:
for your mortgage broker

310.

I don't know how to use
my inner monologue.

311.

I can't think of a song
for my first dance.

312.

My best friend knows
how to fix a car.

313.
I'm still living
la vida loca.

314.
I'm an anarchist.

315.
I believe it is what's
on the <u>outside</u>.

316.

My assistant handles that kind of stuff.

Perfect excuse:
at a power lunch

317.
What happened
in Vegas didn't stay
in Vegas.

318.
It's too exhausting.

319.
It's too expensive.

320.

It's just so much work.

321.

I'm too successful.

322.

I'm waiting
for Guffman.

323.

My favorite person
to hang out with
is me.

Perfect excuse:
at a dinner party no one told
you would be all couples

324.
All the good ones
are married or gay.

325.
I've got a good thing
going with this single
thing and I don't want to
rock the boat.

326.
I don't compete
for guys.

327.
I won't fake-laugh
at stupid jokes.

328.
I don't get along with
other people's parents.

329.
I'm the eternal wingman.

330.

No comment.

Perfect excuse:
for the press

331.

I'm protestin g.

332.

I can't give it the
attention it deserves.

333.

I always do the opposite
of what I'm told.

334.
I'm still
way too immature.

335.
I brag . . . a lot.

336.
I can always be someone
else's plus-one.

337.

World Peace is my
only priority.

Perfect excuse: for the
overly friendly, all-up-in-your-
business, neighborhood barista

338.

We're living longer now,
so I have plenty of time.

339.

I'm putting it off
until next year.

340.

I don't want to be
a statistic.

341.
I have an unwanted
hair problem.

342.
I have common **sense**.

343.
I haven't found anyone
good enough.

344.

I don't know how to nag.

Perfect excuse:
for your smug **married** friends

345.
I'm running a marathon instead.

346.
I'm not supposed to date for at least 12 months after being sober.

347.
I missed the first wave.

348.

I've given myself
to the Lord and am
becoming a nun.

349.

I've got the geek squad.

350.

I've seen the odds.

351.

I get bored quickly.

Perfect excuse:
at a speed dating **event**

352.

I'm so deep, nobody can get through all my layers.

353.

The more I get to know someone, the less I like them.

354.

I'm not ready to change my relationship status on Facebook.

355.

I have shoulders like
a linebacker.

356.

I have the raw materials,
I just haven't figured out
what to do with them yet.

357.

I'd rather be
gardening.

358.

The last guy I dated
was well-endowed
and ruined me for
all other men.

Perfect excuse:
for your ex-ex boyfriend

359.
I don't believe in it.

360.
I need more "me" time.

361.
It's more of
a scheduling issue
than anything else.

362.

I'm waiting for
the fat lady to sing.

363.

I'm 100% too awesome
to settle down.

364.

I forgot.

365.

I complete ME.

Perfect excuse:
for just about anywhere